GUATEMALA

COUNTRY EXPLORERS

Shannon Knudsen

Lerner Publications Company • Minneapolis

Lerner Publications Company
A division of Lerner Publishing Group, Inc.
241 First Avenue North
Minneapolis, MN 55401 U.S.A.

Website address: www.lernerbooks.com

Library of Congress Cataloging-in-Publication Data

Knudsen, Shannon, 1971–
    Guatemala / by Shannon Knudsen.
        p.   cm. — (Country explorers)
    Includes index.
    ISBN 978–0–7613–6412–2 (lib. bdg. : alk. paper)
    1. Guatemala—Juvenile literature. I. Title.
F1463.2.K58 2011
972.81—dc22   2010031158

Manufactured in the United States of America
1 – VI – 12/31/10

Table of Contents

Welcome!

Let's take a trip to Guatemala! This country is in Central America. Central America is part of the continent of North America.

Belize sits east of Guatemala. So do Honduras and the Gulf of Honduras. It is part of the Caribbean Sea. El Salvador lies southeast of Guatemala. The Pacific Ocean touches Guatemala's southern coast. Mexico sits to the north and the west.

Water from the Pacific Ocean washes the western shores of Guatemala.

4

MILES

0   25   50   75

0   25   50

KILOMETERS

Caribbean Sea

Guatemala

equator

MEXICO

SAN PEDRO RIVER

USUMACINTA RIVER

NORTHERN PLAIN

LAKE PETÉN ITZÁ

❖ Tikal

● Flores

BELIZE

GULF OF HONDURAS

GUATEMALA

SARSTÚN RIVER

LAKE IZABAL

DULCE RIVER

POLOCHIC RIVER

HONDURAS

GUATEMALAN HIGHLANDS

TAJUMULCO

MOTAGUA RIVER

LAKE ATITLÁN

SAN PEDRO

TOLIMÁN

ATITLÁN

● Antigua

★ **Guatemala City**

PACAYA

PACIFIC LOWLANDS

N

EL SALVADOR

PACIFIC OCEAN

🌋	mountain
🌋	volcano
▬	plains/lowlands
▬	highlands
🌳	rain forests
★	country's capital
●	city
❖	ancient ruins

Down Low

Guatemala's land is low and flat near the Pacific Ocean. This area is called the Pacific Lowlands. Farmland takes up a lot of the lowlands. The area also has large cattle ranches.

Farm fields cover Guatemala's Pacific Lowlands.

Northern Guatemala has thick tropical rain forests. These forests are disappearing. People have destroyed large areas of trees. But Guatemala's government looks after parts of the rain forests. The government doesn't let people cut down trees in protected areas.

Map Whiz Quiz

Take a look at the map on page 5. Trace the outline of Guatemala onto a sheet of paper. See if you can find the Gulf of Honduras. Mark this side of the map with an *E* for east. Do you see Mexico? Mark this side of the map with a *W* for west. Next, see if you can find the Pacific Ocean. Color the Gulf of Honduras and the Pacific Ocean blue. Use a green crayon for the land of Guatemala.

Animals such as this howler monkey live in Guatemala's rain forests.

7

Up High

Southern Guatemala has many mountains. A mountain range called the Guatemalan Highlands stretches from east to west across the country. Most people live in the south's high valleys.

Four boys walk to school in this village tucked in the Guatemalan Highlands.

8

Red-hot lava pours out of the volcano Pacaya.

Guatemala has thirty-seven volcanoes. Most of them have not blown up in hundreds of years. Others are still active. Sometimes they shoot out lava or ash.

Tajumulco

Western Guatemala has the highest mountain in Central America, the volcano Tajumulco. Tajumulco stands 13,845 feet (4,220 meters) above sea level. It hasn't blown up for more than one hundred years. Climbers who reach the top of Tajumulco can see for many miles.

A black iguana relaxes on a branch. Black iguanas can grow to more than 3 feet (1 m) in length.

Unusual Animals

Guatemala is home to more than twelve hundred kinds of animals. Animals such as the Guatemalan black iguana and the Maya mouse live only in Guatemala. Many animals have lost their homes because of damage to rain forests. Guatemala's government also works to protect forest animals.

A Treasured Bird

The national bird of Guatemala is the resplendent quetzal. *Resplendent* means "shiny" or "dazzling." The quetzal is both! It has bright green and red feathers.

Water Everywhere

Water is easy to find in Guatemala. Long rivers flow across the country. The Motagua River rises in the highlands and empties into the Gulf of Honduras. Lake Izabal is the country's largest lake. It also drains into the gulf. Lake Atitlán is the deepest lake in Central America.

The Motagua River runs from west to east across southern Guatemala.

Heavy rain is common in Guatemala. The country is rainiest from May to November. In some places, rain falls most days of the year.

A fisher hauls in a catch on Lake Atitlán.

Early Peoples

The Maya were some of the first people to live in Guatemala. Almost half of modern-day Guatemalans have ties to the Maya. Most live in small villages and on farms. They follow many Mayan traditions.

These Mayan girls *(bottom row)* wear the colorful, woven clothing of their ancestors.

A Very Old City

The ruins of a Mayan city called Tikal stand high in northern Guatemala. Thousands of Maya once lived in Tikal. The Maya abandoned it about one thousand years ago. Modern-day explorers have found tombs, temples, and Mayan artwork in the ruins.

The ancient Mayan city of Tikal is in northern Guatemala.

A Spanish Colony

Soldiers from Spain came to Guatemala in 1523. They took land and power from the local people. The Spanish started a settlement called a colony. For almost three hundred years, Guatemalans lived under Spanish rule.

Spanish rulers built the original Saint Joseph Cathedral in Antigua around 1514.

Spanish settlers had families with local people. About half of all modern Guatemalans are part native Central American and part Spanish. We call them Ladinos.

A Ladino girl smiles out the side of a train window.

Different Voices

Spanish is the official language of Guatemala. Most Ladinos speak Spanish. But Guatemalans speak more than twenty other languages. Many people in small villages speak forms of the Mayan language. They may learn Spanish too. But some rural Guatemalans never learn Spanish. They don't need to use it.

This modern Mayan family lives in rural Guatemala.

Family Words

Here are the Spanish words for family members.

grandfather	abuelo	(ah-BWAY-loh)
grandmother	abuela	(ah-BWAH-lah)
father	padre	(PAH-dray)
mother	madre	(MAH-dray)
uncle	tío	(TEE-oh)
aunt	tía	(TEE-ah)
son	hijo	(EE-hoh)
daughter	hija	(EE-hah)
brother	hermano	(ehr-MAH-noh)
sister	hermana	(ehr-MAH-nah)

City Life

About half of Guatemala's people live in cities. Guatemala City is the country's capital and largest city. It is home to more than two million people. Most of them are Ladinos.

High-rise buildings dot the skyline of Guatemala City.

Guatemala City has museums, libraries, and sports stadiums. People go to restaurants and concerts. But city life can be hard. Many families in Guatemalan cities are poor. Some neighborhoods are unsafe because of crime.

A man reads a newspaper on a busy street in Guatemala City.

Many Kinds of Homes

In the country, some houses are made of wood. Others are made of adobe. This is a mixture of clay and straw. Many houses have dirt floors. Some houses have no running water or electricity.

This family lives in an adobe house. Many rural houses are made of this traditional material.

Brick houses line the streets in the city of Solola.

Homes are different in Guatemala's cities. There, apartment buildings tower high on busy streets. In smaller cities, people also live in houses. Almost everyone has electricity and running water.

Work, Work, Work

About half of Guatemalan workers are farmers. They grow coffee beans, bananas, cotton, and sugarcane. Most farmers don't own much land. They work on huge farms that others own. Farmers also raise crops at home to feed their families or to sell at markets.

Guatemalans work on a large coffee farm in the Guatemalan Highlands.

In the cities, many Guatemalans are service workers. They cook, clean, or take care of yards. Some people also work in factories. They make clothes, paper, and food products. Other Guatemalans work in offices and stores.

A woman in Antigua runs her own organic restaurant.

Faith

The Spanish brought the Roman Catholic religion to Guatemala. More than half of all Guatemalans are Catholic.

Altar boys help out during a Catholic church service called Mass.

Many Guatemalans are Protestant too. Some people follow parts of the Catholic or Protestant faith and the traditional Mayan religion.

Let's Eat!

Corn is an important food in Guatemala. Dried corn can be crushed into cornmeal. People use cornmeal to make round, flat tortillas. People eat tortillas with beans and chili peppers.

A woman and her granddaughter shell corn to be ground into cornmeal.

28

Celebrate!

Guatemala gained freedom from Spain on September 15, 1821. Every September 15, Guatemalans celebrate Independence Day. City streets fill with crowds. Families watch parades and fireworks.

Kids march in an Independence Day parade.

Dough called masa comes from cornmeal. Guatemalans stuff masa with cheese, meat, or vegetables. They wrap it in a corn husk and steam it to make tamales. People take the corn husks off tamales before eating them.

Lunchtime!

For most Guatemalans, lunch is the biggest meal of the day. Farmworkers eat right in the fields. Their families often bring lunch to them.

In the cities, many stores used to close for lunch. Workers went home for a long meal. Cars clogged the streets at lunchtime. Whole cities slowed down! These days, most stores stay open.

Women at this shop prepare tortillas, fish, beans, and more for lunch customers.

29

The Day of the Dead takes place on November 1. On this day, Catholic Guatemalans honor loved ones who have died. They fly huge kites and decorate graves. They also eat fiambre, a special salad made of meats and vegetables.

Brightly decorated graves mark this cemetery during Día de los Muertos, or Day of the Dead.

31

School or Work?

Most kids in Guatemala start school when they are seven years old. They study reading, writing, math, and history. Children must go to school until they turn thirteen. But some families need children to help earn money instead. Kids from these families sell candy or other foods.

Schoolchildren at this school near Lake Atitlán learn about computers.

In the country, some children have no schools near their homes. These children work in fields, take care of animals, or watch over their younger sisters and brothers.

Rural kids may not attend school if they are needed to help out on the family farm.

Playtime

Guatemalan children have fun in lots of different ways. City kids love TV and video games. In the country, kids play games outdoors. Families who live close to the beaches and lakes enjoy picnics by the water. Brave teens and grown-ups go surfing, rafting, or mountain climbing.

Schoolgirls share a laugh in Guatemala City.

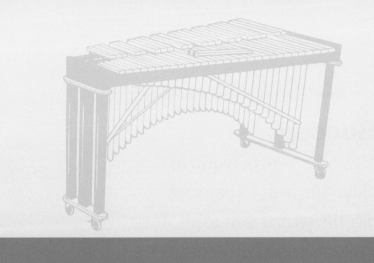

Dear Aunt Amy,

Today we went to a city in a lake! The city is called Flores. Flores is in northern Guatemala. Workers built Flores on an island in Lake Petén Itzá. Flores is old. The streets are made of large, bumpy stones. The houses have red roofs made of tin. Tomorrow we're going to see the Mayan ruins at Tikal. Mom says I can climb up a pyramid there!

Love,
Erika

You_
You_
Anyu_

Flores Island

Lots of Soccer

Guatemalans love soccer. The country's best team is known as Los Rojos. Their nickname is Spanish for "the Reds." They have millions of fans. But so do Los Cremas, the second-best team. Their nickname means "the Creams." Both teams play in Guatemala City. When the Reds face the Creams, the whole city watches!

Schoolgirls in Flores play soccer during a break.

Carlos Ruiz (*in yellow*) kicks the ball past a defender. In 2010, Ruiz played for the Greek team Aris Thessaloniki.

An Amazing Athlete

Carlos Ruiz grew up playing soccer in Guatemala City. He joined Los Rojos as a teenager in 1995. In 2002, Ruiz went to the United States to play. He won the Major League Soccer (MLS) championship with the Los Angeles Galaxy. Ruiz was named the MLS Most Valuable Player. Later he played for a Greek team. Ruiz has also played for the Guatemalan national team. This team competes with teams from other countries.

Walls of Art

Guatemala's most famous painter is Carlos Mérida. He lived during the 1900s. Mérida painted shapes in unusual ways. He also made murals—giant paintings that covered whole walls. Museums all over the world show Mérida's work.

Visitors to the Graciela Andrade de Paiz museum in Guatemala City view artwork by Carlos Mérida.

38

A Guatemalan Hero

Rigoberta Menchú *(left)* is the daughter of a Mayan farm family. She grew up in the 1960s and 1970s. Many people were upset with Guatemala's government at this time. The army often killed people who stood up to the government. Menchú wrote about the wrongs of the government. She risked her life. Menchú won the international Nobel Peace Prize in 1992.

Marimba Music

The marimba is a popular instrument in Guatemala. A marimba is very big. It is made of wooden bars on a stand. Players hit the bars with sticks called mallets.

Musicians at a hotel in Guatemala play the marimba.

If you fly to Guatemala, you may hear a marimba when you get off the plane. Bands often greet travelers at the airport.

Costumed dancers take part in the *Rabinal Achí.*

A Mayan Play

The *Rabinal Achí* is a Mayan play from the 1400s. It tells the story of two princes. Masked actors dance, play music, and speak in poems. People in the town of Rabinal still put on the *Rabinal Achí.* The play is important to people with a Maya background. The play comes from a time before the Spanish arrived in Guatemala.

Made by Hand

Guatemalans make crafts with local materials. Some people weave cloth from cotton and wool. Weavers also make baskets. Other people make pottery, jewelry, and furniture.

These Mayans hold colorfully woven fabrics at a market in Chichicastenango.

Most Mayan weavers are women. They make cloth with bright stripes, shapes, and patterns. Weavers use some cloth for a loose shirt called a *huipil*. The colors and shapes of a huipil tell where a woman is from. Each Mayan village has its own pattern.

No Worries

Worry dolls are a famous craft from Guatemala. These small, colorful dolls are made of cloth or wood. People say that if you tell your worries to a worry doll, it will do your worrying for you!

43

THE FLAG OF GUATEMALA

Guatemala's flag has three wide stripes. The blue stripes stand for the bodies of water on each side of Guatemala. The center stripe is white. The center of the flag shows the country's coat of arms. Laurel branches around the coat of arms stand for peace. A quetzal sits above a rifle, two swords, and a scroll. The weapons stand for strength. The scroll marks the date of Guatemala's freedom from Spain.

FAST FACTS

FULL COUNTRY NAME: Republic of Guatemala

AREA: 42,042 square miles (108,889 square kilometers), or slightly more than the state of Virginia

MAIN LANDFORMS: the Guatemalan Highlands, the Northern Plain, and the Pacific Lowlands; the lakes Atitlán, Izabal, and Petén Itzá; the volcano Tajumulco

MAJOR RIVERS: Dulce, Motagua, Polochic, San Pedro, Sarstún, Usumacinta

ANIMALS AND THEIR HABITATS: Maya mice, jaguars, spider monkeys, quetzals, tapirs, toucans (rain forests); nurse shark, manatees (ocean); crocodiles (rivers)

CAPITAL CITY: Guatemala City

OFFICIAL LANGUAGE: Spanish

POPULATION: about 13,550,440

GLOSSARY

ancestor: a family member who lived long ago

colony: a place where people from another country settle. A colony is controlled by the home country of the settlers.

continent: any one of seven large areas of land. The continents are Africa, Antarctica, Asia, Australia, Europe, North America, and South America.

map: a drawing or a chart of all or part of Earth or the sky

masa: dough made from cornmeal

mural: a large piece of art that covers a wall

poncho: a cloak shaped like a blanket

rain forest: a warm, thick jungle that receives large amounts of rain

tortilla: a round, flat pancake made from cornmeal

tradition: something that people in a particular culture pass on to one another

volcano: an opening in Earth's surface through which hot, melted rock shoots up. Volcano can also refer to the hill or mountain of ash and rock that builds up around the opening.

weave: to make cloth from threads of cotton, wool, or other materials

TO LEARN MORE

BOOKS

Jolley, Dan. *The Hero Twins: Against the Lords of Death.* Minneapolis: Graphic Universe, 2008. Twin boys match their skills against the gods in an ancient Mayan ball game.

Lowery, Linda, and Richard Keep. *The Chocolate Tree: A Mayan Folktale.* Minneapolis: Millbrook Press, 2009. This fun, illustrated book tells the Mayan legend of how chocolate came to Earth.

Takacs, Stephanie. *The Maya.* New York: Children's Press, 2003. Learn more about the modern Maya and their ancestors in this photo-illustrated book.

Walker, Sally M. *Volcanoes.* Minneapolis: Lerner Publications Company, 2008. Check out this book to find out why volcanoes erupt and how they affect human life.

WEBSITES

The Internet Bird Collection: Resplendent Quetzal
http://ibc.lynxeds.com/species/resplendent-quetzal-pharomachrus-mocinno
Visitors to this site can view photos, watch videos, and listen to a recording of Guatemala's national bird.

Journey through Tikal
http://www.destination360.com/tikal/guide.htm
View a map and photos of the ruins of the ancient Mayan city, as well as photos of the treasures found there.

INDEX